A MARRIAGE WITHOUT REGRETS

"AND SO THEY LIVED HAPPILY EVER AFTER!"

What happened to yesterday's fairy tale ending? Today we're living every other "ending," a time when marriage is devalued, minimized, trivialized, even scorned. The commitment to stay married in spite of poverty, sickness, and "worse" things has been replaced with "so long as it works well for me!" Fuses are short, anger long and bitter. Separation and divorce are rampant. Alternatives like "living together" last only a short time. Warring genders seek out their own sex for comfort (homosexuality). Children are major liabilities many prefer to do without.

Why has our culture abandoned marriage? There's a simple answer to this. Our society has rejected marriage because it has rejected the God of truth who created not only the covenant of marriage but also the very genders to enter into the contract. Today these truths and principles of God's eternal Word are rejected, mocked, belittled, or just plain ignored. And we've inherited all the heartache, isolation, regret, guilt, loneliness and hopelessness that accompany the rejection of a personal God. We're alienated first from God and then from each other.

It doesn't have to be this way in your life, beloved. The eternal Word we turned away from is the way out—the path to not just a marriage but also a life without regrets. Jesus said "I am the way, and the truth, and the life; no one comes to the Father but through me" (John 14:6).

I took this "way" a long time ago and have never looked back. Following it entails courage to swim upstream, go against the grain, reject status quo. It means taking a stand against a culture that has taken particular aim at God's first two covenants—life and marriage. It means defying majority belief, standing up for absolutes in a relativistic culture.

God promises more than just "no regrets." Jesus said He came so that his sheep "may have life and have it abundantly" (John 10:10). That means abundant marriages too, abundant relationships generally, a new family, a new future, a new you.

If you're married or are planning to marry, I know you want a marriage without regrets, an abundant marriage filled with love, trust, hope and great memories. I have a lot to share with you because I failed miserably the first time around when I was an unbeliever. Jesus changed all that; He raised me out of the living death I was "living." Join me in this study of His Word. Let's renew our hope together!

Kay

PRECEPTS FOR LIFE™
Study Guide

This Bible study material was designed for use with the TV and Radio teaching program, Precepts for Life™ with renowned Bible study teacher Kay Arthur, a production of Precept Ministries International. This inductive 30-minute daily Bible study program airs on many satellite, cable, and broadcast stations, and on the internet at **www.preceptsforlife.com.**

As with all Inductive Bible studies, the best way to use the material is to complete the assignments in each lesson before listening or watching the PFL program for that day. These programs are also available on DVD and CD at **www.preceptsforlife.com** or by phone (1.800.763.1990 for television viewers or 1.800.734.7707 for radio listeners). For more information about the Precept Inductive Bible Study Method and Precept Ministries International, visit **www.preceptsforlife.com.**

These materials are also useful for Bible study apart from the Precepts for Life™ programs. We hope you'll find them valuable for studying God's Word and that your walk will be strengthened by the life-changing Truth you'll encounter each day.

A Marriage Without Regrets STUDY GUIDE
Published by Precept Ministries of Reach Out, Inc.
P. O. Box 182218
Chattanooga, TN 37422

ISBN–13: 978-1-62119-415-6

PROGRAM 1 — Introduction

TODAY'S TEXT

Genesis 1:26-28

Revelation 4:11

1 Corinthians 8:5-6

Genesis 2:7; 2:18-21

Galatians 3:28

1 Corinthians 11:7-12; 11:3

1. Read Genesis 1:26-28 marking *man* and all pronouns with a black stick figure.

   a. What in the text tells us that "man" is not Adam only? (Carefully check the use of all pronouns.)

   b. From this fact, what can we say about male and female? Are they equal or unequal? Are they both made in God's image?

2. Now read Revelation 4:11. Did God want to create you? What do you think He wants from you?

3. Now read Genesis 2:7, 18, and 19-21.

   a. What did God make the male out of according to v. 7?

   c. What did God fashion the woman out of? Is this part of the body significant as compared to others He could have used?

4. Now read 1 Corinthians 11:7-12. What are the man and the woman respectively the glory of?

5. Finally, read 1 Corinthians 11:3.

   a. Who is the head of every man?

   b. Who is the head of the woman?

PROGRAM 2 — Differences of Men and Women

TODAY'S TEXT

Genesis 2:23

1 Peter 3:7

1. Read Genesis 2:23.

   a. Why was Eve called "woman?"

   b. What does "out of" imply in terms of rank and/or equality?

2. Now read 1 Peter 3:7. (See the NASB's marginal note for "someone weaker.")

   a. In what ways are women "weaker vessels"?

   b. Among other reasons, why are men to honor their wives according to this verse? What are they in God's eyes? Is this a temporal or eternal honor? Which of the two has the higher rank?

PROGRAM 3 — Purpose of Marriage

TODAY'S TEXT

Genesis 1:28

Hebrews 13:4

Ephesians 5:25-32

Deuteronomy 22:28-29

1. Read Genesis 1:28. What are God's purposes for marriage according to the text? List the verbs.

2. Now read Hebrews 13:4.

   a. How does a couple keep their marriage bed "undefiled"?

   b. According to the text, why don't options to marriage work?

3. Read Ephesians 5:25-32.

   a. How are husbands supposed to love their wives?

   b. What did Jesus do for His Church that a husband should do for his wife?

4. Finally, read Deuteronomy 22:28-29. If a man seizes a virgin who is not engaged and lies with her,

   a. What does he have to do?

   b. What can he never do?

PROGRAM 4 — The Master Key

TODAY'S TEXT

Mark 8:31-34

Luke 14:26

Ephesians 4:31—5:2

1. Read Mark 8:31-34.

   a. What was Peter trying to do? Can we save our loved ones?

   b. How did Jesus respond to Peter's attempt?

2. Now read Luke 14:26.

   a. How is a person to hate "his own life"? How can we reconcile this with Jesus' command to love our neighbors as ourselves?

   b. Who should be our first love?

3. Finally, read Ephesians 4:31—5:2.

   a. Does 4:31 help us understand hating our own "soul" (the old man)?

   b. Who are we called to "imitate"?

PROGRAM 5 — Lies That Women Believe

TODAY'S TEXT

2 Timothy 3:16

2 Peter 1:20-21

Psalm 12:6

1 Timothy 5:14

Titus 2:3-5

1. Read 2 Timothy 3:16, 2 Peter 1:21, and Psalm 12:6. Mark all the characteristics of the *Word of God* with a purple open book shaded green and then list them here.

2. Now read 1 Timothy 5:14 red underlining what Paul commends the *younger women* to do. List these things here:

3. Finally, read Titus 2:3-5 red underlining what Paul commends the *older women* to do and red shading the two "*so that*"s. List his commendations here:

Did you know...

you can watch or listen to *Precepts For Life*™ whenever you wish? You can even download the programs to build your Bible study library or share with a friend.

Visit www.PreceptsForLife.com to study online—on your time.

PROGRAM 6

More Lies That Women Believe

TODAY'S TEXT

Proverbs 6:26-32; 7:25-27

CROSS REFERENCES

Leviticus 20:10

1. Read Proverbs 6:26-32 marking *harlot* with a red "H" and *adulteress* and its respective synonyms, pronouns, and associated terms which refer to her with a red "A".

   a. What's the huntress's preference, a wealthy or poor man? What does harlotry lead a man to?

   b. What two images does Solomon use to show that harlotry has bad results that are inevitable?

2. Now read Proverbs 7:25-27 shading the female pronouns that refer to the adulteress (from v. 5) with a red "A".

   a. What do you think the "ways" and "paths" of an adulteress are?

   b. Why is the adulteress's way/path dangerous? What happens to her "victims"?

PROGRAM 7

Essential Factors for a Marital Foundation

TODAY'S TEXT

Genesis 2:22-25

Ephesians 5:22-33

1 Corinthians 11:3; 7-9

Matthew 19:3-12

Romans 7:2-3

CROSS REFERENCES

1 Corinthians 6:16

1. **Stewardship.** Read Genesis 2:22-25 marking *man* and respective pronouns with a stick figures.
   a. Did God give Eve to Adam? What verb implies this?
   c. What accountabilities to the woman does the man have?

2. **Identification.** Now read Ephesians 5:22-33 marking *love(s)(d)* and associated terms with a red shaded heart. How is a man to love his own wife?

3. **Headship.** Read 1 Corinthians 11:3 and then 7-9 red underlining all terms related to rank.
   a. How do the three headships in v. 3 help us explain what "head" means?
   b. What is the woman "the glory" of?

4. **Permanence.** Read Matthew 19:3-12 marking *divorce* plus synonyms and pronouns with two overlapping side-by-side circles with a black line through them. Then read Romans 7:2-3. What does Jesus say about divorce? What does the Law "say" compared to what Moses "permitted."

5. **Unity.** Now re-read Genesis 2:24, Matthew 19:5-6 and **Cross-reference** 1 Corinthians 6:16 marking *one flesh* and *one body* with a red number 1. What unity is God seeking in a marriage?

6. **Transparency.** Re-read Genesis 2:25. What do the terms in the phrase *naked and not ashamed* imply with respect to the man, the woman, and God?

PROGRAM 8	**The Fruit of Disobedience**

TODAY'S TEXT

Genesis 3:6-16

CROSS-REFERENCES

John 6:5-6

Psalm 22:1

Habakkuk 1:13

Genesis 4:7b

Song of Solomon 7:10

1. Re-read Genesis 3:6-16 marking man , woman, and respective synonyms (e.g. husband)—but not pronouns—with different stick figures.

   a. What happened to the man and woman after they ate the fruit from the tree of the knowledge of good and evil?

   b. What did they do?

   c. Were the man and woman able to hide from God successfully?

   d. What does the Lord connect the nakedness and hiding with according to v. 11?

   e. What two punishments did the Lord mete out to the woman?

PROGRAM 9	**Why Happiness Eludes the Modern Woman**

TODAY'S TEXT

Genesis 2:23

1 Peter 3:7

1. Re-read Genesis 3:1-5, 14, 22 marking the *devil* and all synonyms and pronouns with a red pitchfork.

   a. Who speaks to the woman in these verses?

   b. According to Genesis 3:4, what did he tell Eve?

   c. What else did he tell her according to verse 5? What this true? (See 3:22.)

2. Now review Titus 2:3-5 underlining all good characteristics of godly women. List them here. What primary purpose for these qualities does Paul have in mind?

PROGRAM 10 — How To Be An Excellent Wife

TODAY'S TEXT
Proverbs 31:10-31

Read Proverbs 31:10-31. List all the features of the "excellent wife" by Virtue (e.g. "trustworthy" in v. 11) and Action (e.g. "works with her hands" in v. 13 but notice that "in delight" is a virtue). Some of these will be derivative: for example a woman who rises early to work and works hard has the virtue "industrious."

Virtues	Actions

Concerned you might miss a program?

Don't be! You can get a CD or DVD of this program and mark the Observation Worksheets as you study at your own pace. It will be like going to God's Bible school and having the Holy Spirit as your professor. He will take the things of God and reveal them to you.

TV viewers, call 1.800.763.1990, radio listeners, call 1.888.734.7707! We'll be happy to place an order for you!

You can also listen to or watch the programs online whenever you want on our website **www.PreceptsForLife.com.**

PROGRAM 11	**Older Women, Younger Women, Widows**

TODAY'S TEXT

1 Timothy 5:1-16

1. Read 1 Timothy 5:1-3 underlining **_widow_** and shading _godly qualities/actions_ for widows one color and _ungodly qualities/actions_ another (your choice).

   According to verses 1-3 how are believers generally supposed to treat

   a. Older men?

   b. Younger men?

   c. Older women?

   d. Younger women

   e. Widows?

2. Now read 5:4-16 repeating the marking/shading above.

   a. Who is responsible for caring for parents?

   b. List the characteristic(s) of

      1) the godly widow specified in verse 5:

      2) the ungodly widow specified in verse 6:

PROGRAM 12	**What God Says About A Model Man**

TODAY'S TEXT

Genesis 1:1, 28

Daniel 4:35

1 Corinthians 11:3

John 3:16

Ephesians 5:25

Philippians 4:19

1 Timothy 5:8; 3:1-13

Titus 1:5-9

1. Read the following pairs of scriptures, then for each: title the role man plays in a marriage that reflects God's attribute.

   a. _____ Genesis 1:26, 28

   b. _____ Daniel 4:35; 1 Corinthians 11:3

   c. _____ John 3:16; Ephesians 5:25

   d. _____ Philippians 4:19; 1 Timothy 5:8

PROGRAM 13

How To Be The Man You Want To Be

TODAY'S TEXT
1 Timothy 3:2-4

CROSS-REFERENCES
Ecclesiastes 3:1-8
Philippians 3:12
1 Timothy 5:10
Hebrews 13:2
Ephesians 6:4
Deuteronomy 6:7

Read 1 Timothy 3:2-4. Review and list the qualifications for an overseer.

PROGRAM 14

Contrast A Model Man and An Evil Man

TODAY'S TEXT
Titus 1:5-9, 12
2 Timothy 3:1-2

CROSS-REFERENCES
Isaiah 1:2-4
Titus 1:12
Joshua 1:8
2 Timothy 4:7-8
1 Corinthians 11:1

1. Read Titus 1:5-9, 12 and list the primary characteristics of a leader.

2. Now read 2 Timothy 3:1-2. List the characteristics of the wicked in "the last days."

PROGRAM 15 — Four Different Kinds of Love

TODAY'S TEXT

Romans 1:31

2 Timothy 3:3

Proverbs 30:16 (LXX)

Luke 7:6

Luke 20:46

John 5:20

John 11:11

John 15:14-15

Matthew 5:46

Luke 11:43

John 3:16

John 3:35

1. στοργη (*storge*). Read the following verses. Write in the English term. Then check the context to discover the terms this adjective is associated with.

   a. Romans 1:31 (The negative *astorgos* = not-storge, the 3rd term in the verse)

   b. 2 Timothy 3:3 (The negative again, here the 1st term in the verse)

2. ἔρως (*eros*). This term is found only in the Septuagint (LXX) version of Proverbs 30:16 which speaks of the "eros of a woman" as something that, among the other things listed, is "never satisfied." The term is used extensively in other Greek writings from Homer forward. We derive our English word erotic from this Greek term.

3. φιλος (*philos*). Read the following verses to discover the English term that most frequently translates this "love" term which is often found in compound form in Greek and English: *philosophy* (love of wisdom), *philadelphia* (love of brethren), etc.

   a. Luke 7:6

   b. Luke 20:46

   c. John 5:20

   d. John 11:11

   e. John 15:14-15

4. ἀγάπη (*agape*). We'll be studying this extensively next week. For now, read the following verses and see if you can determine the meaning of this frequently used Greek term for "love":

   a. Matthew 5:46

   b. Luke 11:43 (compare with 20:46 above)

   c. John 3:16

   d. John 3:35 (compare with 5:20 above)

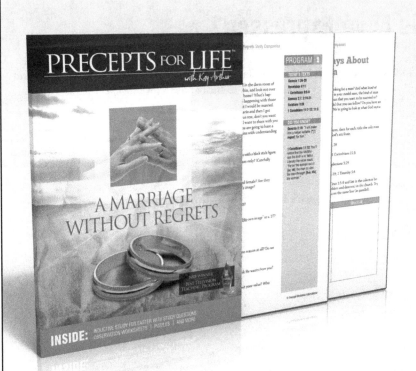

PROGRAM 16 — Unconditional Love

TODAY'S TEXT

Jeremiah 31:3

John 3:16

1 John 4:7, 9, 10, 19

1. Read Jeremiah 31:3, marking every noun *love* ♥ and every verb form (*love, loves, loved, loving*) with a red heart.

   a. How is God's love for Israel (v. 2) characterized?

   b. How far back does it go?

2. Now read John 3:16, marking every *love* as above.

   a. How does "only begotten" value God's love?

   b. How does "gave" value God's love? Was this love conditional or unconditional? If conditional, what was it conditioned on?

3. Finally, read 1 John 4:7, 9, 10, and 19, marking every *love.*

   a. What is the source of love?

   b. What is the connection between "born of God" and love?

PROGRAM 17 — How is Love Expressed?

TODAY'S TEXT

Matthew 19:19

Ephesians 5:25

1 John 4:7

1. Review God's general command to us to love (*agape*) one another in Matthew 19:19 and 1 John 4:7 and then His specific command to husbands to love (*agape*) their wives in Ephesians 5:25.

2. For each of Kay's four "expressions" of *agape* from her program, given below, list examples of things you can do.

Love consists in making another person feel

   a. Comfortable

   b. Special

   c. Appreciated/praised (responding to love from others)

PROGRAM 18 — Essentials For Communication

TODAY'S TEXT

Proverbs 18:21

James 3:3-12

Ephesians 4:29

Genesis 2:23-25; 3:11

CROSS-REFERENCES

Colossians 4:6

Matthew 19:6

Ephesians 5:25, 33

1. Read Proverbs 18:21 marking *tongue* and pronouns with a megaphone.

   a. What two fruits is the tongue capable of producing?

   b. How do you want to use your tongue? Who should you use it for?

2. Read James 3:3-12. Continue to mark *tongue* as above.

   a. What things is the tongue compared to in this section?

   b. Even though these things are small what kind of effects do they produce per the text?

3. Read Ephesians 4:29 and cross-reference Colossians 4:6. In 4:29 mark the phrase ***word proceed from your mouth*** with a megaphone.

PROGRAM 19 — Ministry of Communication

TODAY'S TEXT

Proverbs 17:17

Proverbs 18:21

Matthew 7:1, 2

Romans 2:1

James 4:11

Romans 12:10

James 1:19

1 John 3:18

CROSS-REFERENCES

2 Corinthians 3:7

Matthew 12:36-37

1. Read Proverbs Proverbs 18:21 and **Cross-references** 2 Corinthians 3:7 and Matthew 12:37.

   a. What two powers are in the tongue? Is there a gray or neutral area between these two? Do you think every categorical judgment we speak has either life or death attached to it?

   b. Why are our words so significant according to Jesus in Matthew 12:36-37?

2. List James' three exhortations in James 1:19, note how each improves communication, write out what you plan to do with each tomorrow and who you think will be most impacted.

   a. Quick to _____

   b. Slow to _____

   c. Slow to _____

PROGRAM 20 — Art of Communication

TODAY'S TEXT

Romans 15:7

Proverbs 15:4; 18:14

Ephesians 5:29; 4:15

2 Timothy 2:24

Proverbs 15:1; 16:21; 15:28

Colossians 4:6

Proverbs 16:24; 19:11

Read **Today's Texts,** then complete the columns below for the two categories, Speech and Attitude. We did the first one for you.

VERSE	GOOD TONGUE	BAD TONGUE
Proverbs 15:4	Soothing tongue—Tree of life	Perverse tongue—crushes spirit

VERSE	GOOD ATTITUDE	BAD ATTITUDE
Romans 15:7	Accepting others (praise)	Rejecting others (criticism)

PROGRAM 21	Dorie—Unloved and Unwanted

TODAY

Kay's guest today is Dorie N. Van Stone (1st of 3 programs).

Enjoy Kay's interview of Dorie N. Van Stone, author of *No Place to Cry: The Hurt and Healing of Sexual Abuse* and *Dorie: The Girl Nobody Loved.*

PROGRAM 22	Importance Of Our Words

TODAY

Kay's guest today is Dorie N. Van Stone (2nd of 3 programs).

Enjoy Kay's continuing interview of Dorie N. Van Stone.

Then, as Kay suggests, go to the Gospel of John and begin to read it.

  1. Mark every occurrence of the word *love* with a heart.

  2. Every occurrence of the word *life.*

List what you learn. You'll find out how to have life and how to know the love of God that will hold you and transform you and keep you and will never leave you or forsake you.

You are precious to God! Let Him show you how precious you are!!

PROGRAM 23 — Healing After Sexual Abuse

TODAY

Kay's guest today is Dorie N. Van Stone (3rd of 3 programs).

Enjoy Kay's concluding interview of Dorie N. Van Stone.

If you haven't finished, continue marking *love* and *life* in the Gospel of John and listing what you learn.

Finally, list some thoughts from the following verses about the connection between forgiveness, cleansing from sin, and healing:

2 Chronicles 7:14

Jeremiah 30:16-20

Jeremiah 33:6-22.

PROGRAM 24 — "Nevers" in Communication

TODAY'S TEXT

2 Corinthians 5:19

Proverbs 19:11; 13:10

Ephesians 4:26

James 1:19-20

Matthew 7:12

Proverbs 18:14

Ephesians 4:29

Job 16:4, 5

Proverbs 17:9

John 13:35

Proverbs 17:27; 13:15; 14:29-30

THE "NEVERS" *(Read all the listed verses)*

1. **Never** say "never" or "always" with respect to bad attitudes or actions: "You'll never change; you'll always be the same."
   1 Corinthians 5:19.
   1) How does Paul qualify (define) "reconciliation" here?
   2) If we extend this attitude and action toward people, how will it help communication with them?

2. **Never** accuse a person of a feeling or attitude.
   Proverbs 13:10. What's a major cause of strife? How do we do it? How does it wreck good communication?

3. **Never** disallow someone's feelings.
   Ephesians 4:26. Can we stop negative emotions like anger from flaring up? Can we regulate them?

4. **Never** attack character.
   Matthew 7:12. What general approach to people does Jesus commend?

5. **Never** counterattack.
   Proverbs 17:9. What love-action is described here? How does it aid good communication?

6. **Never** discuss in anger.
   Proverbs 17:27. Write out the two qualities of a good communicator.

7. **Never** stop or discontinue a discussion.
   Proverbs 13:15. Describe the two pre-communication attitudes here and explain how they help or hinder good communication.

PROGRAM 25 — What God Says About Sex In Marriage

TODAY'S TEXT

Genesis 2:22-24

1 Corinthians 6:13-16

Genesis 1:28

Proverbs 5:15-19

1 Corinthians 7:1-5, 26-27

CROSS-REFERENCES

Hebrews 13:4

1. Review Genesis 2:22-24 and compare with 1 Corinthians 6:13-17.

    a. If a man plans on living with a woman, what should he do according to Genesis 2:24? List the actions and explain what each entails specifically.

    b. What are we "members" of? If a man "joins himself to a prostitute is he "married" to her in God's eyes?

2. Now read Genesis 1:28 and Proverbs 5:15-18.

    a. What is the *primary* purpose for sex?

    b. List the phrases in the Proverbs passage that emphasize the exclusivity of the sexual relation in marriage.

3. Read 1 Corinthians 7:1-5, 26-27.

    a. What is one reason for a man to have a wife?

    b. Do husbands and wives have sexual duties to each other? How does "duty" relate to "pleasure"? Are husbands and wives bound to pleasure their spouses even if the act doesn't please them?

PROGRAM 26 — How to Have Good Sex in Marriage

TODAY'S TEXT
Job 31:1
1 Corinthians 6:12-7:9

1. Read Job 31:1.

   a. What does this verse have to say to someone who argues that marriage is "just" a piece of paper, or a wedding, or living together?

   b. What is it, truly?

   c. Who is it directed to—the Lord, the spouse, witnesses?

2. Now review 1 Corinthians 6:12—7:9 shading every reference to **body** in yellow.

   a. Again, what did God design our bodies "for" according to 6:13?

   b. Does Paul make a point about bodily pleasure *generally* in the first part of the verse? If so, could we read sexual (as opposed to hunger) categories into it? What's Paul's major point in *the context*?

PROGRAM 27 — What God Says About Sex Outside of Marriage

TODAY'S TEXT
Leviticus 20:7-8, 10-21; 18:6-25

1. Read Leviticus 20:7-8, 10-21, and 18:6-25.

   a. Contrasted with the nations that did whatever they wanted, what did God call Israel to do with respect to His statutes according to 20:7-8?

   b. Compile a chart of sexual sins. Be sure to list before them the verse reference(s).

PROGRAM 28 — Consequences of Immorality

TODAY'S TEXT

Romans 1:21-27
Proverbs 6:23-35; 7:6-27

1. Read Romans 1:21-23. List the things that happen to the minds and hearts of those who do not honor God or give him thanks.

2. Now read vv. 24-25.

   a. What does God do to these people?

   b. What are their lusts redirected toward?

3. What's next in the chain of depravity according to vv. 26-27?

4. Review Proverbs 6:23-35 and 7:6-27.

   a. What risk do the adulterer and adulteress take?

   b. How does this danger compare with the bad consequences in Romans 1?

PROGRAM 29 — How Do You Handle Temptation?

TODAY'S TEXT

2 Samuel 11:1-27
Job 31:9-12
Matthew 5:27

CROSS-REFERENCES

1 Corinthians 6:18

1. Read 2 Samuel 11:1-27.

   a. How many times should David have "stopped" in his progression toward adultery and follow-up sins?

   b. Where would you say he "tempted his own flesh"? Is this a good idea?

   c. What mental and physical sins was David guilty of apart from adultery?

2. Now read Job 31:9-12.

   a. What does Job wish on himself if he has not been loyal to his wife?

   b. What kinds of punishment does the adulterer receive?

3. Finally read Matthew 5:27 and **Cross-Reference** 1 Corinthians 6:18.

   a. Is adultery only physical?

   b. What is Paul's counsel to the Corinthians?

PROGRAM 30 — What Do You Do After You've Yielded to Temptation?

TODAY'S TEXT

2 Samuel 11 (Lesson 29)

1 John 1:9

Proverbs 28:13

2 Corinthians 7:8-10

James 4:1-2

1. Review Lesson 29—David's adultery with Bathsheba and murder of Uriah the Hittite—with respect to how he handled these sins as they accumulated.

2. Now read 1 John 1:9.

   a. What two things will God do when we confess our sins to Him?

   1) _____

   2) _____

3. Read Proverbs 28:13.

   a. What happens to those who conceal their sins?

   b. What happens to those who confess and forsake their sins?

4. Read 2 Corinthians 7:8-10.

   a. What are the characteristics of "sorrow according to the will of God"?

   b. What are the characteristics of "sorrow of the world"?

5. Now read James 4:1-2.

   a. What causes quarrels and conflicts?

   b. What can unsatisfied lust lead to?

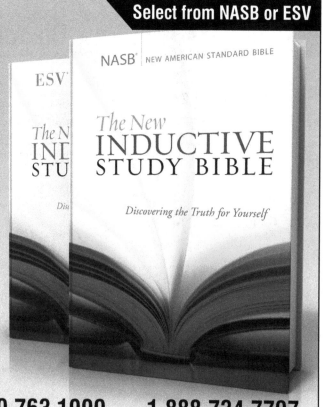

PROGRAM 31 | Temptation—Consider the Cost

1. Review Lesson 29 again.

2. Now let's see what happened to David. Read 2 Samuel 12:1-14.

   a. Why did David get so angry when he heard this story?

   b. What did Nathan accuse David of? Besides Uriah and Bathsheba who else were damaged by David's sins?

   c. What three terrible judgments does Nathan pronounce on David? While David attempted to sin in secret, was God going to judge him in secret?

      1)

      2)

      3)

   d. How did David respond to this pronouncement? Did these judgments impact Israel as a nation in the long run? If so, how?

PROGRAM 32 | The Do's and Don'ts When You Are Tempted

1. Review God's judgments on David in 2 Samuel 12:10, 11, 14.

   a. Did David's sin "find him out" (Numbers 32:23)? Can we sin "undercover" against God? Can we ever "get away with it"?

   b. If you're familiar with Israel's subsequent history, how did God's "sword" in David's house work out shortly after Solomon's reign? What did David personally suffer?

2. Now read Psalm 73:1-20.

   a. Did Asaph have a moral problem with the present status of rich people?

   b. Briefly summarize his thoughts about the long-term future of the rich. Should the wealthy consider such thoughts? Why or why not?

3. Now read James 1:13-15.

   a. Is temptation sin? Is lust sin?

   b. What source of David's temptation was he responsible for?

4. Finally, read the account of Joseph and Potiphar's wife in Genesis 39:5-13.

   a. What had Pharaoh put Joseph in charge of?

   b. What did Potiphar's wife do to entice Joseph?

   c. Did this "end well" for Joseph?

   d. Is it always easy to take a stand for God's precepts against persevering evils? What occasions are the most difficult?

PROGRAM 33 — When You Commit Adultery

TODAY'S TEXT

Exodus 20:14

Malachi 2:10

Genesis 15:9-12, 17-18

Galatians 5:16, 22-24

1 Corinthians 6:18

1 Thessalonians 4:3-6

1. Read Exodus 20:14.

   a. Is adultery optional for the believer?

   b. Who's saying "No!" to it here?

2. What do you learn about God's covenant with Israel from the following:

   a. Malachi 2:10?

   b. Genesis 15:9-12, 17-18?

3. Now read Galatians 5:16, 22-24.

   a. What ethical advantages does a believer have according to vv. 16 and 24?

   b. List the nine qualities of the one fruit of the Spirit. Check off the ones you think especially help to offset and overcome sexual lust.

4. Review 1 Corinthians 6:18 and read 1 Thessalonians 4:3-6.

   a. What is the believer to specifically "flee" and why?

   b. What is the will of God for the believer?

PROGRAM 34 — How To Approach God After You Have Sinned

TODAY'S TEXT

Psalm 51:1-12

Leviticus 17:11

1 Peter 1:18-19

Hebrews 9:22; 10:29

1 John 1:7

Hebrews 11:6

Exodus 34:6

1 John 1:8-9

CROSS-REFERENCES

James 4:12

1. Read Psalm 51:1-12.

   a. What attributes of God does David appeal to in v. 1 for God to blot out his sins?

   b. Who do we sin against ultimately (v. 4)? Why do you think? (See **Cross-reference** James 4:12 for a hint.)

   c. List the *ways* David asks God to save him.

2. What do the following tell us about *whether* and *what* we must believe about God in order to please Him?

   a. Hebrews 11:6

   b. Exodus 34:6

3. How do we deal with sin after we've been born again according to 1 John 1:8-9?

PROGRAM 35 — Wash Me, Cleanse Me O God

TODAY'S TEXT

Psalm 51:1-12

Leviticus 14:1-7

Isaiah 1:16-18

John 13:8-10; 10:10; 6:37

Hebrews 9:12; 10:10; 10:14

CROSS-REFERENCES

Hebrews 13:11-13

1. Review Psalm 51:1-12. Summarize the three segments using the titles Kay gave to each:

   a. vv. 1-2: _____

   b. vv. 3-6 _____

   c. vv. 7-14 _____

2. Now read Isaiah 1:16-18.

   a. What does God command His people to do generally?

   b. Does He give specific examples of what He wants them to do?

3. Read John 13:8-10.

   a. Why do you think Peter did not want Jesus to wash his feet? What's the *general* problem? Is this a problem for us today?

   b. How did Jesus respond to Peter? Was this a threat?

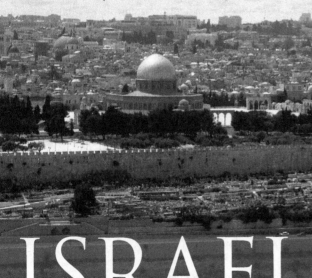

PROGRAM 36 — What Does God Require For Forgiveness?

TODAY'S TEXT

Psalm 51:1-18

Jeremiah 13:11

Ephesians 1:13-14

Hebrews 13:5-6

Romans 5:1-8

1. Review Psalm 51:1-18.

   a. What was the occasion for David writing this Psalm?

   b. List what David asks God <u>not</u> to do *to* him.

   c. List what David asks God to do for him.

2. From the following verses, what do we know about the Lord and about what He has done to secure our relationship with Him?

   a. Ephesians 1:13-14

   b. Hebrews 13:5-6

   c. Romans 5:1-8

PROGRAM 37 — When You Have Sinned Against God

TODAY'S TEXT

Psalm 51:1-18

1. Review Psalm 51:1-18. Find the verses that contradict the statements that follow. Then write in the verse number and key terms or phrases underneath.

   a. _____ God only *partially* washes off iniquity.

   b. _____ God wants us to be believers "on the outside" only.

   c. _____ The best we can hope for is a gray mix of good and bad attitudes and actions.

   d. _____ The Lord doesn't gift us with perseverance; that's something we have to do ourselves.

   e. _____ We can bury sins deep enough in our subconscious so they won't bother us.

   f. _____ Salvation is dull (more than one here).

   g. _____ We can lose God's anointing and ministries permanently.

   h. ___ I don't need God's power to praise (worship) Him.

PROGRAM 38 — Untangling the Mess When Your Mate Has Committed Adultery

TODAY'S TEXT

Ezekiel 16:5-8, 32

Jeremiah 2:2, 20-25

Jeremiah 3:2

Deuteronomy 24:1-4

Matthew 19:9

1 Corinthians 7:15

1. Review the following verses. After each, briefly summarize God's "been-there, done-that" experience with His own adulterous wife, Israel.

   a. Ezekiel 16:5-8, 32

   b. Jeremiah 2:2, 20-25

2. Read Deuteronomy 24:1-4.

   a. If a man divorces his wife and she remarries, if her second husband rejects her, can her first husband take her back?

   b. Why or why not?

3. After each verse, write a key term that describes the exception that permits divorce.

   a. Matthew 19:9 _____

   b. 1 Corinthians 7:15 _____

PROGRAM 39 — My Mate Has Committed Adultery. How Can I Forgive?

TODAY'S TEXT

Jeremiah 3:12-13

Ephesians 4:26

Ezekiel 16:25, 59-62

Ephesians 4:31-32

Luke 23:34

Matthew 6:12, 14

Matthew 18:21-35

1. Read Jeremiah 3:12-13.

   a. What does God command his "faithless" people?

   b. What does He promise and on what basis (attribute)?

   c. What does He "only" demand of them?

2. Now read Ezekiel 16:25, 59-62.

   a. Who did Israel, God's wife, attempt to seduce?

   b. What does God threaten to do?

   c. Is this threat and punishment permanent? What does He further promise to do farther down the road?

3. Now read the entire parable in Matthew 18:21-35.

   a. What did Peter ask?

   b. How did Jesus respond?

   c. How do the two debts compare?

   d. How does Jesus conclude the parable in v. 35? Just how important is forgiveness? By analogy, how much do we "owe" God compared to what others "owe" us?

PROGRAM 40 — Practical Steps For Reconciliation

TODAY'S TEXT

2 Corinthians 2:6-7

1 Corinthians 13:5

Proverbs 17:9

Ephesians 5:12

Proverbs 19:11

Ecclesiastes 9:9

2 Corinthians 10:4

Philippians 4:8

1. Read 2 Corinthians 2:6-7.

   a. Is it possible to over-punish someone for a past sin?

   b. What should we do instead?

2. According to 1 Corinthians 13:5, what four characteristics of love are peculiarly aimed at reconciliation? Are these easy to "pull off"?

3. Read Proverbs 17:9. Write down the actions that correspond to the motives noted:

   a. Seeks love by _____

   b. Separates intimate friends by _____

4. Read Proverbs 19:11.

   a. What does a man need to restrain his anger?

   b. What is one "glory" he should pursue? How?

6. According to 2 Corinthians 10:4 are we "on our own" in dealing with life's harshest situations? How does the Word of God help us deal with the worst?

7. What should we put our minds on according to Philippians 4:8?

Did you know...

that you can walk more closely with God by studying with others? People are meeting in small group studies and church Sunday school classes in all 50 states—and there's probably one near you. Want to join them?

Find a group near you—TV viewers call 1.800.763.1990, radio listeners call 1.888.734.7707, or visit www. PreceptsForLife.com.

DISCOVER TRUTH FOR YOURSELF

Our passion is for you to discover Truth for yourself through Inductive Bible Study—a unique Bible study method you'll

discover in the following pages and use throughout this study, as we engage this important topic together verse by verse.

You can't do a better thing than sit at Jesus' feet, listening to His every word. God's Word, the Bible, has answers for every situation you'll face in life. Listen to what God is saying to you, face-to-face, with truth to transform your life!

INDUCTIVE BIBLE STUDY METHOD

To study and understand God's Word, we use the Inductive Bible Study Method at Precept Ministries International. The Bible is our main source of truth. Before looking for insights from people and commentaries *about* the Bible, we get into the Word of God, beginning with observing the text.

❶ Observation

This is a very interactive process, well worth the time because the truths you discover for yourself will be accurate and profound. It begins by asking the five W and H questions.

Who is speaking? Who is this about? Who are the main characters? And to whom is the speaker speaking?

What subjects and/or events are covered in the chapter? What do you learn about the people, the events, and the teachings from the text? What instructions are given?

When did or will the events recorded occur?

Where did or will this happen? Where was it said?

Why is something said? Why will an event occur? Why this time, person, and/or place?

How will it happen? How will it be done? How is it illustrated?

Careful observation leads to interpretation—discovering what the text means.

❷ Interpretation

The more you observe, the greater you'll understand God's Word. Since Scripture is the best interpreter of Scripture, you and I will be looking at contexts and cross-references to enhance our understanding of the meaning of God's message.

Where should observation and interpretation lead? Application.

❸ Application

After we've observed the text and discovered what it means, we need to think and live accordingly. The result is a transformed life—the more you and I are in the Word of God and adjusting our thinking and behavior to its precepts for life, the more we are changed into the likeness of Jesus Christ! He is the living Word of God who became flesh, the Savior of the world, our coming King of kings!

SO WHERE DO YOU BEGIN?

The Bible is *God's* book, His Word, so when you study it you need to seek the Author's help. Begin with prayer, asking God to lead you into all truth, then open the Study Companion. (We suggest you work one program ahead of the broadcast to get the most out of the study.) Look at the general layout of each day's program and you will find the following:

- Introduction—usually with a challenging question
- Questions that contain pointers on using the Inductive Bible Study Method
- **Where's That Verse?** section containing the Primary Study Passage and several cross-references related to the topic
- Concluding Prayer

WHAT'S NEXT?

- In some programs, I'll point out key words to mark. You'll find many of them on the back cover of this Study Companion with *suggested* colors and symbols to spot them quickly in the text. Color coding key words helps you identify and recall. We have included a cutout bookmark so you can remember to mark each key word the same way throughout the text.

  You can mark these key words before or after the program, whichever is easier. You can also get the CD or DVD of the program and mark the key words later while studying.

Feel free to mark them your own way—there's nothing sacred about the particular symbols and colors I use!

- The cross-references I mention in these programs are under **Where's That Verse?** After you read them, you can jot them in the margins of the **Observation Worksheets** or write them in the wide margins of your Bible. I suggest you first pencil them in, then write them in ink later.

- For book studies, you'll find an **At A Glance** chart in the back. After we complete a chapter, record a summary theme there and in the space provided in your **Observation Worksheets**. Themes help you remember main ideas of chapters **At A Glance** after you finish the study. You'll also find these charts after each book in the *New Inductive Study Bible*.

MISSED A PROGRAM?

- Go to our website at **www.PreceptsForLife.com**. TV viewers can call 1.800.763.1990 and radio listeners 1.888.734.7707 to learn how to find programs online.

GETTING THE MOST FROM THIS STUDY

- Try to stay one program ahead of me so you'll learn directly from the Word of God and our time together will be like a "discussion group," as we reason together through the Scriptures. You'll get much more out of our time together if you've done this preparation.

- Try to memorize a key verse for every program covered. God will bring these to your remembrance when you need them!

- Pray about what you learn each day. Ask God to remind you of these truths and give you another person to share them with. These two exercises will do amazing things in your life.

- Get the CD or DVD set of this series and listen when you get ready for work in the morning, do chores around the house, or have family devotions. Or listen with an open Bible and discuss the teaching and its application to your life. Get together with a friend, view or listen to a message, and discuss it or use it for family devotions. You can also view or listen programs online. Visit **www.PreceptsForLife.com.**

- Request Precept's mailings to stay abreast of what God is doing around the world and to pray for the needs we share with you. You can be a significant part of this unique global ministry God is using to establish people in His Word. Here are some items you can request:

◆ The *Plumbline*—Precept Ministry's monthly e-newsletter that keeps you up to date on Bible study topics, products and events that help you in your walk with Christ.

◆ A prayer list so you can partner with us in prayer for our ministries in nearly 150 countries and 70 languages.

◆ "Inside information" each month when you join our "E-Team" of regular prayer and financial supporters. Visit **www.PreceptsForLife.com** for more information on how you can support our programs. (You can check out the current monthly letter right now on our website.)

◆ Advance notice of conferences at our headquarters in Chattanooga and throughout the United States and Canada.

◆ Information about our study tours in Israel, Jordan, Greece, Turkey, and Italy, where we teach various books of the Bible right where the action occurred!

• We use one of the most accurate translations of the Bible, the New American Standard (Updated). If the topic is a book study, our **Observation Worksheets** will contain the complete text. Since you'll be instructed to mark words and phrases and make notes in the text, you'll want to have colored pencils or pens available. As you grow in inductive study skills, you may want to use your Bible instead. We believe the best Bible to use is the *New Inductive Study Bible.* See our back pages to find out more about this ultimate study Bible. Now get started!

• Finally, stay in touch with me personally. I'd so love to hear from you by email or letter so I can be sensitive to where you are and what you're experiencing—problems you're wrestling with, questions you have, etc. This will help me teach more effectively and personally. Just email us at info@precept.org. (Don't worry, Beloved, I won't mention you by name; but as you listen, you'll know I've heard you!)

I'm committed to you . . . because of Him. The purpose of the "Precepts For Life" TV & Radio programs is to help you realize your full potential in God, so you can become the exemplary believer God intends you to be…studying the Bible inductively, viewing the world biblically, making disciples intentionally, and serving the Church faithfully in the power of the Holy Spirit."

That's my vision for us as believers! Won't you help us spread it to others?

Looking for people…looking for truth!

How Do I Start Studying The Bible?

Do you wonder,
God, how can I obey You and study your Word? Where do I begin? How can I discover truth for myself?

DISCOVER TRUTH FOR YOURSELF

There are some study tools we would recommend for you to begin with, as each will teach you the inductive method of study. By inductive we mean that you can go straight to the Word of God and discover truth for yourself, so you can say … "for You, Yourself have taught me" (Psalm 119:102).

Let's Get Started! For a jump start on inductive study, we recommend the following:

- *Lord, Teach Me To Study The Bible in 28 Days.* In this hands-on introduction to the basics of inductive study, you'll see why you need to study God's Word and how to dig into the truths of a book of the Bible. The instructions will walk you through the books of Jonah and Jude, and you'll be awed at what you see on your own! Discussion questions are included.

- *God, Are You There? Do You Care? Do You Know About Me?* This 13-week, self-contained inductive study on the Gospel of John is powerful and life-changing. Study the book of John, as you learn and put into practice inductive study skills. The Gospel of John was written that you might believe that Jesus is the Son of God and that believing, might have life in His name. You will know you are loved! Discussion questions are included.

- *How to Study Old Testament History and Prophecy Workshop.* Discover truths about who God is and how He works as you learn to study inductively, step by step, and be challenged to apply these truths to your life. This workshop will give you the tools to study and understand Old Testament history and prophecy. Go to www.precept.org or call 800-763-8280 to find out about workshops in your area, or online training.

- *How to Study a New Testament Letter Workshop.* Grow in the knowledge of the Lord Jesus Christ and His plan for your life. This inductive study workshop will equip you to study the New Testament letters and apply their truths to your life. Go to www.precept. org or call 800-763-8280 to find out about workshops in your area, or online training.

Now that you've begun . . . continue studying inductively using one of these:

- *40 Minute Bible Studies.* These 6-week topical studies are a good for personal study and a great way to start discipling others one-on-one or in a group setting—teaching them who God is, introducing them to Jesus Christ, and helping them learn God's precepts for life. These studies enable you to discover what God says about different issues of life. No homework is necessary for the students prior to group time.

- *The New Inductive Study Series,* now complete covering every book of the Bible, was created to help you discover truth for yourself and go deeper into God's precepts, promises and purposes. This powerful series is ideal for personal study, small groups, Sunday school classes, family devotions, and discipling others. Containing 13-week long studies, the New Inductive Study Series also provides easy planning for church curriculum! You can now survey the entire Bible

- *Lord Series.* These life-changing devotional studies cover in greater depth major issues of our relationship with God and with others, teaching us how to practically live out our faith. Ideal for small groups, these contain discussion guides and teaching DVDs are available for some.

- *Discover 4 Yourself* is a dynamic series of inductive studies for children. Children who can read learn how to discover truth for themselves through the life-impacting skills of observation, interpretation, and application. You'll be amazed at the change that comes when children know for themselves what the Word of God says! Teach them now so they can stand firm in a first-hand knowledge of truth as they hit their teen years. This award-winning series is popular in Christian schools and among homeschoolers. Teacher's guides are available online.

- *The New Inductive Study Bible (NISB)* is a unique and exciting! Most study Bibles give you someone else's interpretation of the text. The NISB doesn't tell you what to believe, rather it helps you discover truth for yourself by showing you how to study inductively and providing instructions, study helps, and application questions for each book of the Bible, as well as wide margins for your notes. It's filled with many wonderful features that will guide you toward the joy of discovering the truths of God's Word for yourself. This Bible is your legacy.

GO DEEPER WITH OTHERS... IN SMALL GROUP BIBLE STUDIES

Join others in the study of God's Word, sharing insights from the Scripture and discussing application to your life. Each of the studies described above are appropriate for groups as well as for individual study.

Discussion questions are included, so that you can dialogue about what you're learning with a group. These studies will teach you what it means to live by God's Word—and how it is applied to life. Learn about and discuss with others the truth that sets you free! To find out about inductive Bible study groups in your area, go to www.precept.org or call 800-763-8280.

DISCIPLE

How can you help others study God's Word inductively? Use the studies described above to share with others—one-on-one or in a small group. Lead others in discovering truth for themselves and experience the joy of seeing God change lives!

If you want training in how to lead these and other Precept Upon Precept studies go to www. precept.org or call us at 800-763-8280.

Precept Ministries International | P.O. Box 182218 | Chattanooga, TN 37422
800.763.8280 | www.precept.org

CPSIA information can be obtained
at www.ICGtesting.com
Printed in the USA
LVHW061120231119
638270LV00027B/552/P

9 781621 194156